CW00408555

Quodlibet

A Q-Rated Encyclopaedia

Illustrations by Katja Spitzer
Text by Sebastian Gievert
Translation by Dr. Michael Routledge

Q
James Bond's gadget man

Q which stands for 'Quartermaster' is a character in the world of the secret agent, James Bond, created by the British writer, Ian Fleming. Q, played by Desmond Llewelyn, works for the British foreign intelligence service, MI6, and is responsible for providing 007 with technical equipment. Amongst his best-known gadgets are a crocodile-shaped submarine, a fountain pen containing a mixture of nitric and hydrochloric acid (*Octopussy,* 1983), an umbrella with a deadly

steel point (*For Your Eyes Only,* 1981) and 'Dentonite' toothpaste with C4 explosive (*Licence to Kill,* 1989). In Q's garage there are sports cars with rocket launchers, ejector seats and machineguns. Q often equips Bond with watches, which incorporate useful tools such as saws, laser beams, direction finders, Geiger counters, winches and telex machines. Q's inventions almost always end up being destroyed by Bond when he uses them.

Qi Baishi
20th-century Chinese painter

Qi Baishi (b.1864–d.1959) is regarded as the master of modern Chinese painting. He came from a poor peasant family and, after an apprenticeship in carpentry, began painting at the age of twenty. In his forties he travelled around China and, at the age of about 60, set up a studio in Beijing. His paintings, achieved with a small number of brush strokes, are mainly lifelike representations of small creatures such as crabs, shrimps, tadpoles, mice, birds and

frogs, or fruits such as bananas and pumpkins or flowers such as lotuses and peonies, and everyday objects. Qi Baishi depicted human figures in a style that was often naïve and occasionally humorous. The name 'Qi Baishi' roughly translates to 'white cliff'. He exhibited his paintings under pseudonyms such as 'The Old Man of the Mountain' or 'The Old Man of the Apricot Bank'.

Qilin
Chinese unicorn

Qilin   a unicorn-like creature in Chinese Mythology which foretells the birth or advent of a wise ruler and betokens being blessed with children and good fortune. Unlike the European unicorn, which has the body of a white horse, its outward appearance varies. A qilin usually has the shape of a stag or an ox. Its body is completely covered with scales. Its head is like that of a dragon but with fangs and the antlers of a deer, a beard and goggle eyes. Despite its

predatory appearance, legends depict the qilin as a peaceable creature that lives in the forest with other animals. It is exclusively vegetarian and can walk on grass without disturbing the structural integrity of a sinlge blade. However, as the servant of a wise judge, it impales criminals and sinners upon its horn. During the Chinese Qing dynasty high-ranking officers wore robes with qilin motifs, the symbol being synonymous with justice.

Quack
Charlatan or unqualified doctor

Quack is a term for people who, although they have no training, sell medical services or medicines to the sick. The idea of fraudulent intent or ineffectiveness is often attached to the term, and they are also known as 'charlatans'.

In the Middle Ages quacks often travelled around amongst roaming bands of merchants, shouting their wares from fairground booths, for example. Still today, the Austrian Society of Apothecaries publishes 'Ten Rules' to avoid being taken in by

quacks. Quacks can be found as motifs in the history of art. The term may come from the Dutch (kwakken – to quack like a duck, or to deliver a 'spiel') or from the idea of 'quicksilver', which, in early modern times, was a favourite, but ineffective, remedy for syphilis. Having said that, some quack remedies have been found to contain effective ingredients. One, willow bark, contains salicylic acid, a naturally occuring equivalent of the active component of asprin.

Quack grass or Quitch
Weed

Quack grass a member of the *gramineae* family is one of the most tenacious weeds in western Europe. Also known as 'couch grass', this weed grows to a height of between 20 and 150 cm, appears on arable land or fertile meadows and can cover large areas. Once quack grass has a hold, it is very difficult to eliminate. Mechanical approaches are useless: the roots of quack grass reach several metres deep into the ground and send out widely branched runners. If just one

piece remains in the soil a new plant will spring up from it. Farmers used to burn quack grass to the ground but these days pesticides are the preferred approach. Quack grass is also known as 'quick grass' from which its etymology is most likely derived. In folk medicine it is used as a diuretic and for cleansing the blood. It is purported to help with inflammation of the urinary tract and to dissolve kidney stones.

Quadrille
Ballrooom dance

The quadrille is a French ballroom dance. It originated in the 18th century in Paris during the time of Napoleon. Popular variations on the quadrille are the can-can and the square dance. The original quadrille was danced at an energetic pace and was boisterous and rapid. The dancers flung their arms and legs about ecstatically, and moved around enthusiastically in lively, ever-changing formations. The high point was the moment when one of the female

dancers placed a well-aimed kick that knocked her partner's hat from his head and then did the splits. In the 19th century a quadrille, danced at midnight, was the climax of any ball. Johann Strauss famously composed the *Fledermaus* *Quadrille (Op. 363)*. In Lewis Carroll's *Alice in Wonderland*, the Gryphon and the Mock Turtle dance the Lobster Quadrille. 'Quadrille' is also a favourite word in crosswords because it contains so many vowels.

Quagga
Extinct form of the plains zebra

The quagga is a subspecies of the plains zebra that has been extinct since the 19th century. The animal's head is striped black and white, like ordinary zebras, but its body is reddish-brown. These large, odd-toed ungulates were once widespread in South Africa but were hunted to extinction by 1883. There are still some 23 remains of quagga pelts and skeleton fragments around the world, mainly in Germany. The natural history museum in Wiesbaden displays,

as Exhibit Number 442, a stuffed male quagga that dates from 1865. Because, until 1997, it was not displayed in an air-conditioned environment, the flanks of the pelt are now splitting open and the seams coming apart. Since 1987 South Africa's Quagga Project has been attempting to bring back quaggas by selectively breeding ordinary zebras. A foal, Henry, with the closest resemblance to a quagga so far, was born on 20th January 2005.

Quant
Inventor of the mini-skirt

Mary Quant (b. 1934) is a British fashion designer and the inventor of the mini-skirt. In 1955, at the age of 21 she opened her first boutique, *Bazaar,* on London's King's Road. In the 1960s she designed her revolutionary skirts that stopped at least 10 cm above the knee, most even higher. In 1962 her mini-skirt was applauded by *Vogue Magazine,* much to the horror of the conservative establishment. The skirt, along with its typical wearer, a woman with bobbed hair and

1962

↕10cm

1972

1969

a childlike appearance, became a style icon of the 1960s. In 1966 Queen Elizabeth II gave Mary Quant an OBE. In 1969 Quant shortened the mini even further to the micro-mini and, in 1971, invented hot-pants. But Quant's intention had never been to create a sexy look: it was all about freedom of movement for women and setting their legs free: "I was making easy, youthful, simple clothes, in which you could move, in which you could run and jump" said the fashion pioneer.

Quantz
Frederick the Great's flute teacher

Johann Joachim Quantz (b.1697–d.1773) was a German composer, performer and Frederick the Great's flute teacher. His travels took him to France, Italy and many other countries, including England, where he made the acquaintance of Georg Friedrich Handel. He also cultivated a friendship with the castrato singer Farinelli and was a great admirer of Antonio Vivaldi. In 1728 he was appointed as flute teacher to the future Frederick II and in 1741 became his court

composer and chamber musician. Frederick the Great's father, the soldier-king Frederick I, would not allow his son to learn music, preferring to have him taught military drill. Quantz said that, on one occasion when Frederick I was checking up on his son, he had had to hide in a cupboard. Quantz composed more than 500 pieces for flute and improved the instrument's capabilities by using a longer head and foot joint.

Quarter Horse
The fastest horse in the world

Quarter horses are the world's fastest horses and, there are 4.6 million of them, the most numerous of the horse breeds. If a quarter horse gallops from a standing start it will quickly overtake humans (30 kilometres per hour), dogs (40km/h) and antelopes (56km/h). It can reach speeds of up to 88 km/h, although the swordfish (90 km/h), cheetah (110km/h) and peregrine falcon (up to 360km/h in a swoop) would beat it. Its 'cow sense' and good character make

the quarter horse a versatile and much loved animal, especially amongst cowboys. Its name came from the quarter mile races that took place in the USA from the 18th century onwards. These races, often run on nothing more than a 440-yard (about-400 metre) stretch of road and pitched just two horses against each other. Nowadays, instead of horses, souped-up cars are used in quarter-mile races.

Quartet
Card game / group of four musicians

7A   The Beatles
PAUL MC CARTNEY

♥FOOD   Cheese, Chicken
♥DRINK   Milk
♥CLOTHES   Suede Leather
♥STAR   Brigitte Bardot

7B   The Beatles
RINGO STARR

♥FOOD   Steak
♥DRINK   Whiskey
♥CLOTHES   Suit
♥STAR   Brigitte Bardot

Quartet   Derived from the latin word meaning quartus,"the fourth", a quartet is a card game for any number of players. Any four cards that are of the same kind or thematically linked constitute a quartet. Every player has to try to obtain as many thematically linked cards as possible by asking for them. Some of the most popular games are those depicting cars, planes or ships. Ever since the fifteenth century in the field of music, a quartet has meant

a composition for four instruments or voices, and also a group of four musicians. The Beatles and Abba are well-known examples of quartets in pop music. String quartets and wind quartets are instrumental groupings that can include piano, flute and oboe. A concerto in which four instruments take turns to perform a solo is known as a quadruple concerto.

Quattrocento
The 15th-century Italian Renaissance

Quattrocento is the term applied in history, particularly art history, to the 15th century Italian Renaissance. The term is mainly used to distinguish it from the High Renaissance, the Cinquecento. Florence was the hub of the Quattrocento. It was there that the architect Filippo Brunelleschi established the neo-classical style, thereby laying the foundations for the architecture of the new era. The Quattrocento was shaped by the outstanding

talents of artistic visionaries, including the sculptors Lorenzo Ghiberti and Donatello, the painters Paolo Uccello, Fra Angelico, Masaccio, Piero della Francesca, Giovanni Bellini, Andrea Mantegna, Antonio Pollaiuolo, Sandro Botticelli, the architect Leon Battista Alberti, as well as the painters Andrea del Verrocchio and Benozzo Gozzoli. The most important development achieved by the artists of the Quattrocento is considered to be linear perspective.

Queen
The Queens of England

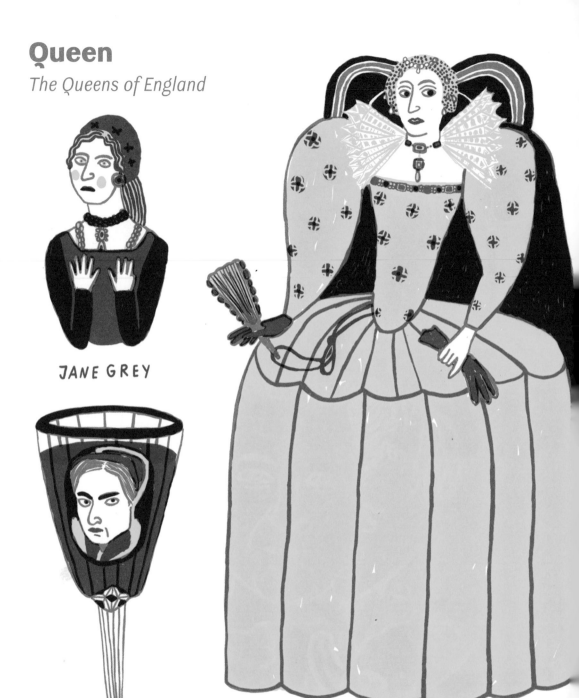

JANE GREY

MARY TUDOR

ELISABETH I.

Queen is the term for all 26 queens of England, of whom seven reigned in their own right. The 'Nine-Day Queen', Lady Jane Grey (Tudor, b. 1527 –d. 1554) was executed by her successor, Mary I (Tudor, b. 1516–d. 1558). Also known as 'Bloody Mary' because of her violent persecution of Protestants, Mary was followed by the 'Virgin Queen' (because she never married), Elizabeth I (Tudor, b. 1533–d. 1603). Later that century protestant Mary II (Stuart, b. 1662–d. 1694) was

MARY II.

ANNE

VICTORIA

ELISABETH II.

succeeded by her sister, Anne (b. 1665–d. 1714). She was the last of the Stuarts and is believed to have given birth to 17 or 18 children, none of whom survived into adulthood. Victoria (Hanover, b. 1819–d. 1901) reigned for 63 years – without her husband, Albert, whom she excluded from affairs of state. The current monarch is Elizabeth II (Windsor, b. 1926) who, on ascending the throne in 1953 said: "It's a job for life".

Queen Alexandra Birdwing
Species of butterfly

The Queen Alexandra Birdwing is a rare butterfly of the *ornithoptera* genus. The yellow-and-black females reach a wing-span of up to 25 centimetres, making them the world's largest butterflies. The males are smaller with iridescent, blue-and-green markings. The species was only discovered in 1906 by Albert Stewart Meek in Papua New Guinea. He shot the butterfly down with a gun because he couldn't catch it with a butterfly net. Meek named his specimen after

the English Queen Alexandra, consort of King Edward VII. Queen Alexandra Birdwings are native to the rainforests of Papua New Guinea's northern province. Their caterpillars almost exclusively eat the aristolochia plant, a form of birthwort that can grow to a length of 40m. Due to its beauty, this butterfly is heavily sought after by collectors and poachers, and was consequently placed on the list of protected species in 1966. It's natural habitat and future hang in a precarious balance.

Queen Charlotte Islands

Canadian archipelago

The Queen Charlotte Islands lie in the North Pacific and belong to Canada. The two main islands, together with 200 other smaller islands, have a total population of about five thousand, of which half are indigenous Haida people. Ninstints, the settlement that they abandoned in 1880, with its traditional longhouses and totem-poles, was declared a World Cultural Heritage Site in 1980. According to their legends, the world was created by a raven, which also taught the Haida how to

build houses. The sacred bird of the indigenous people is said to have stolen this idea from the beaver. Because of their remoteness and the wealth of fauna in their rainforests the Queen Charlotte Islands are sometimes referred to as Canada's Galapagos. The tourist office claims that the climate, with an average temperature of 8°C, is very mild; however, the islands are known for their abundant rainfall.

Queensland Fever (Q-fever)

Infectious disease

Queensland Fever is an infectious disease also known as Q-fever or Query Fever, which can be passed from animals to humans. Sheep are particularly prone to the disease, especially if they have been bitten by ticks. The pathogen can survive for many years in dust, hay or wool and can infect humans in a number of ways, including through inhalation or through skin contact. People working in stockbreeding or in slaughterhouses are at the highest risk

of catching this disease. Infection can cause inflammation of the lungs or liver. In 2004, 250 visitors to a farmers' market who had been admiring a lambing ewe fell ill with the disease. Q-fever was a component of the US biological warfare programme. As recently as 2007, a woman researcher working in a biological warfare laboratory contracted Q-fever.

Queneau
French writer

somehow

Raymond Queneau (b.1903–d.1976) was a French surrealist, editor, film-maker and mathematician, best known for his self-imposed *exercices de style* (exercises in style). He relates a banal event in 99 versions. The scene is Paris, the bus-stop at the Gare Saint-Lazare. A young man is jostled on the S-Line bus. He sits down in an empty seat and later on meets an acquaintance who advises him to have a button sewn higher on his coat. Queneau relates this scene as a sonnet, or other:

a haiku, a book jacket blurb and an interrogation. Queneau became famous when his novel, *Zazie dans le Métro,* was filmed by Louis Malle. Queneau was fascinated by numbers and they often provided the basic framework for his playful and experimental writings. He was a joint founder of the OULIPO language workshop and editor of the *Encyclopédie de la Pléiade*, published by Gallimard.

Quentin Tarantino
Film director

Quentin Tarantino was born in 1963, Knoxville, Tennessee, and grew up on the outskirts of Los Angeles watching kung fu and grindhouse films in suburban cinemas. He left school at 15 and worked as an usher in a porn cinema and then later in a video shop. He later took acting classes and attended Robert Redford's film-making course. Tarantino grew to fame as a director. The outstanding features of his films are the use of stylistic devices taken from martial arts,

spaghetti westerns, B-movies, gore films, and carefully chosen background music. They also regularly feature Red Apple cigarettes, Big Kahuna Burgers, Chevrolets and shots of feet. All his movies were shot on analogue film. His films are so well-known that it would be superfluous to relate their plots. What is less known, however, is that Tarantino appeared in a *Golden Girls* episode as an Elvis impersonator in 1988: the sequence can be found on YouTube.

Quetzalcoatl
Deity

Quetzalcoatl is a Central American deity who was worshipped by the Aztecs and Toltecs, among others. His name derives from the Nahuatl for "feathered serpent." He was lord of the wind, the earth, the heavens, a symbol of the ocean and most importantly he was regarded as the creator-god responsible for the existence of mankind. He is often depicted with a black-painted body and a head-dress of bones. He wears a blue disc which represents the precious

QUETZALCOATL VS TETZCATLIPOCA

liquid *Chalchihuatl:* blood from human sacrifice. He holds before his face a bird mask, decorated with serpents fangs. Other representations show him as a serpent decorated with the precious feathers of the quetzal bird. According to myth, Quetzalcoatl was destroyed and driven from his realm by his brother, catlipoca, whose attributes are sacrificial knives and a jaguar costume, together with an obsidian mirror with which he can see into the future.

Quiche Lorraine
A speciality of French cuisine

Quiche Lorraine is a typically French dish which originated in Alsace-Lorraine but is now enjoyed all over France. It was originally made of bread dough but today short crust pastry is used. There are regional variants such as "Quiche Vosgienne" (with spicy cheese) and "Quiche Alsacienne" (with onions). The classic recipe is as follows: take 250g of flour, 150g of butter, an egg, and a little salt and knead it into a dough. Using a rolling pin, roll

Bon appétit!

it out to a thickness of 1/2 cm, place it into a buttered baking dish and prick it with a fork. Put the dish in an oven preheated to 200°C and bake for 15 minutes. Meanwhile, cut bacon into small pieces and fry it. Mix the bacon with 200ml cream and add salt and pepper. Pour the mixture into the cooked pastry case, and bake for a further 30 minutes. The quiche is best served warm with a fresh, green salad accompanied by a light white wine or cider. *Bon Appétit!*

Quince
Sharp tasting fruit

The Quince is a part of the apple family. One of the oldest varieties in the world, its fruits are apple - or pear-shaped. Their flesh is hard, sour and sharp, and unappetising when raw. The Greek doctor, Hippocrates, recommended preparations of quince as a remedy for diarrhoea and fever. Second century Roman physician and philosopher Galen used quince juice to strengthen the stomach. His recipe has survived using a mixture of quinces, honey,

ginger, pepper and vinegar, which was be taken two hours before eating. In southern Hungary pregnant women eat pieces of quince with drops of blood from a strong man in order to have healthy babies. The drinks manufacturer, Bionade, asked 1001 Germans to name their favourite fruit: quinces came last, with a score of 0.1%. Bionade is using television and radio advertising to create a better image for the fruit since the launch of their quince-flavoured drink.

Quinn, Anthony
Actor

Anthony Quinn (b. 1915, *Chihuahua*, d. 2001, Boston) was an American actor who entered the USA illegally with his mother. He spent his first few years in America in the slums of Los Angeles. To overcome his unfavourable situation, Quinn, who at the outset spoke no English, took a number of jobs, including as a newspaper-seller, shoeshine-boy, bricklayer, street-preacher and boxer. He later got a grant to study architecture under Frank Lloyd Wright. It was Wright who, after

learning of his interest in acting, encouraged
him to pursue it as a career. As an actor he
began by playing bit-parts, usually as an Indian
or a Mexican in westerns. But he rose to greater
success, with the lead roles in *La Strada* (1954)
and *Zorba the Greek* (1965). He twice received
an Academy Award as best supporting actor.
Anthony Quinn was 1.88 m tall, played the
saxophone and became a father for the twelfth
time at the age of 81.

Quito
Capital of Ecuador

Quito, the world's highest capital city, is in Ecuador, in a 2,850 m high river basin in the Andes. Scarcely the ideal place for a settlement, this city of 1.4 million inhabitants is surrounded by 14 volcanoes, standing at the foot of one of them, the Rucu Pichincha. The old town is a World Heritage Site although many of its buildings have been rebuilt several times after devastating earthquakes. According to legend, Quito was founded by Quitumbe, a chieftain. He and his

Sebastián de Belalcázar

partner, Llira, were the only survivors of a flood, having taken refuge in Rucu Pichincha. Archaeological evidence shows that Quito was inhabited from 1500 BC by members of the Cotocollao culture, until the Incas conquered the area in the 15th century. Modern Quito was declared a city in 1556 on the ruins of the former Inca city by Sebastian de Belalcazar. When the republic of Ecuador was formed in 1830, Quito became its capital.

Don Quixote
Literary character

Don Quixote – also known as "The Knight of the Doleful Countenance" – is a character in the novel by the Spanish author, Miguel de Cervantes (b. 1547 – d. 1616). Quixote, a member of the country gentry is deranged by his excessive reading of tales of chivalry, and rides through Spain, believing that he must distinguish himself from his peers by accomplishing heroic deeds. He is accompanied by his squire, Sancho Panza. The best-known episode details his

fight against windmills, which he believes to be giants. *The Ingenious Hidalgo Don Quixote de la Mancha* (published in two volumes in 1605 and 1615) is regarded as the first true novel in world literature. The image of the gaunt Don Quixote and his nag, Rocinante, together with his tubby side kick, Sancho Panza on his donkey, has left its mark on modern culture. In 2005 Spain issued a 2-euro coin with an image of Don Quixote, and there is even an asteroid named after him.

Quoits
Traditional throwing game

Quoits, also known as pitchers, is a game in which players throw rings over a spike. There are countless variations of this game in Great Britain and the USA. The history of quoits is obscure: according to a popular theory the game has its origins in ancient Greece where it was a highly regarded alternative to Olympic discus throwing. Another story has quoits developing out of the pub game 'horseshoes' and yet another version has it the other way round. Under Edward III,

Thomas Jefferson

EDWARD III.

quoits, together with other "useless and time-wasting sports" was banned in order to promote the more practical archery. By the 1700s quoits was regarded as a game for gentlemen. A young lawyer by the name of Thomas Jefferson, of Virginia, records in his diary for June 21st 1769 that he "had lost sevenpence halfpenny playing at pitchers" – Jefferson would later become President of the United States. The first official quoits rules date from 1881.

Quoll

Australian marsupial

Just one more

Quoll is the world's second-largest, carnivorous marsupial. These nocturnal animals, about the size of a cat, are threatened with extinction. Quolls give birth to up to 30 young in a litter but, of these, only a maximum of six survive, because this is the number of teats that the mother has. What is more, adult quolls in Australia have developed a taste for venomous cane toads. These creatures are so poisonous that the quoll population has not learned to

avoid the species, dying before they can learn from their mistakes. Scientists at the University of Sydney have therefore injected cane toads with a substance that causes nausea in quolls. In the study the "toad-savvy" quolls survived up to five times longer than their "toad-naive" counterparts. Study leader Professor Rick Shine found a similar method helpful: "When I was 18 I drank too much Scotch; I'm 60 now and haven't touched a drop of it since."

Illustration: Katja Spitzer
Text: Sebastian Gievert, Katja Spitzer
Translation: Dr. Michael J. Routledge
Editor: Alex Spiro
Typography: Paulina Pysz

Katja Spitzer: Many thanks to Paulina Pysz,
Susanne Koppe and also to Nobrow Press.

Published by Nobrow Ltd. 62 Great Eastern St,
London, EC2A 3QR.

Printed in Belgium on FSC paper.

ISBN: 978-1-907704-21-5

Order from: WWW.NOBROW.NET

Can't wait to get X and Y?
Here's what's in store:

Start collecting now to have your full set!